What's the ATTRACTION?

Elizabeth Raum

Raintree

www.raintreepublishers.co.uk

Visit our website to find out more information about **Raintree** books.

To order:
- ☎ Phone 44 (0) 1865 888112
- 🗎 Send a fax to 44 (0) 1865 314091
- 💻 Visit the Raintree bookshop at **www.raintreepublishers.co.uk** to browse our catalogue and order online.

First published in Great Britain by Raintree,
Halley Court, Jordan Hill, Oxford OX2 8EJ,
part of Harcourt Education.
Raintree is a registered trademark of Harcourt
Education Ltd.

Editorial: Nancy Dickmann and Harriet Milles
Design: Michelle Lisseter and Bigtop
Illustrations: Darren Lingard
Picture Research: Mica Brancic and Maria Joannou
Production: Camilla Crask

Originated by Modern Age
Printed and bound in China by WKT Company
Limited

10-digit ISBN 1 406 20464 1 (hardback)
13-digit ISBN 978-1-4062-0464-3
11 10 09 08 07
10 9 8 7 6 5 4 3 2 1

10-digit ISBN 1 406 20489 7 (paperback)
13-digit ISBN 978-1-4062-0489-6
11 10 09 08 07
10 9 8 7 6 5 4 3 2 1

**British Library Cataloguing
in Publication Data**
Raum, Elizabeth
What's the Attraction - (Fusion): Magnetism
538.3
A full catalogue record for this book is available from
the British Library.

Acknowledgements
The author and publisher are grateful to the
following for permission to reproduce copyright
material: Alamy Images **pp. 14–15** (Bernd
Mellmann); Corbis/Reuters **p. 5**; Corbis/Zefa/
G. Schuster **p. 11**; Getty Images **pp. 27, 29**
(bottom); Getty Images/ Photodisc **pp. 22, 29**
(3rd down); Los Alamos National Laboratory **p. 11**;
Masterfile **p. 9**; NASA/JPL **p. 25**; PhotoDisc **p. 7**;
Redferns/Phil Dent **pp. 20–21, 29** (2nd down); Rex
Features/RESO **p. 22**; Science Photo Library **pp. 6**
(Sinclair Stammers), **16** (Jeremy Walker).

Cover photograph of a horseshoe magnet and iron
filings reproduced with permission of Science Photo
Library/Erich Schrempp.

The publishers would like to thank Nancy Harris and
Harold Pratt for their assistance in the preparation of
this book.

Every effort has been made to contact copyright
holders of any material reproduced in this book. Any
omissions will be rectified in subsequent printings if
notice is given to the publishers.

Disclaimer
All the Internet addresses (URLs) given in this book
were valid at the time of going to press. However, due
to the dynamic nature of the Internet, some addresses
may have changed, or sites may have changed or
ceased to exist since publication. While the author and
publishers regret any inconvenience this may cause
readers, no responsibility for any such changes can be
accepted by either the author or the publishers.

It is recommended that adults supervise children on
the Internet.

Contents

What is a magnet?   4

The first magnetic tools   6

Fridge magnets   8

Powerful pullers   10

Speeding magnets   14

Magnets at work   18

Magnets everywhere   26

Magnet power   28

Glossary   30

Want to know more?   31

Index   32

Some words are printed in bold, **like this**. You can find out what they mean on page 30. You can also look in the box at the bottom of the page where they first appear.

What is a magnet?

You probably use **magnets** every day. Without magnets, your life would be slower. It would be quieter. It would also be a lot less fun!

A magnet is a special piece of metal. It **attracts** certain kinds of metal. These metals pull toward a magnet. They may stick to it. Most magnets are made of **iron** or **steel**. Iron and steel are metals.

The man in the picture calls himself Mr. Magnet. When he puts a fork on his chest, it sticks there. Is he really a magnet? No. Doctors have checked him over. Mr. Magnet just has sticky skin! Only metal objects can be magnets.

attract	pull together
iron	bright, silver-coloured metal
magnet	object with the power to attract things made of iron, steel, nickel, or cobalt
steel	hard, tough metal that contains iron

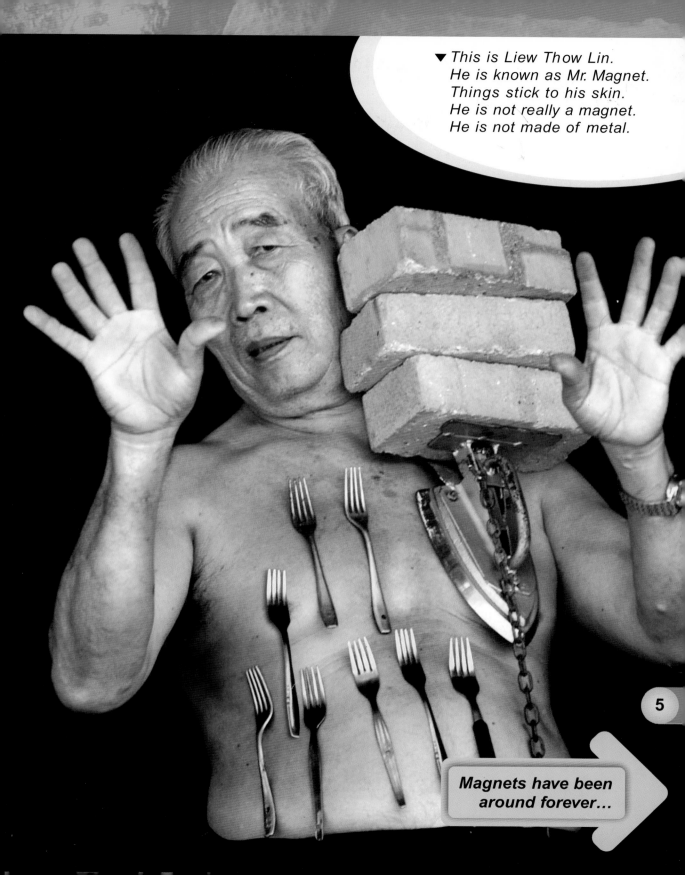

▼ This is Liew Thow Lin.
He is known as Mr. Magnet.
Things stick to his skin.
He is not really a magnet.
He is not made of metal.

Magnets have been around forever...

The first magnetic tools

No one knows who first discovered **magnets**. It may have been people in China or Greece. They found **lodestones** thousands of years ago. Lodestones are special rocks. They are full of **iron**. They have been struck by lightening. This makes them **magnetic**.

This rock is a lodestone. ▲
It is a magnet.

compass   tool that uses magnetism to find direction
lodestone   rock that is a natural magnet
magnetic   something that has the power of a magnet

Greek sailors used a lodestone to make a **compass**. A compass helps people find out which direction is north and which is south. The sailors used a needle-shaped piece of lodestone. They put it on top of an object. The object was floating in a bowl of water. One end of the lodestone pointed north. The other end pointed south.

Compasses showed sailors which direction to travel. Sailors could travel long distances without getting lost. People were amazed by the power of magnets. They found other ways to use magnets.

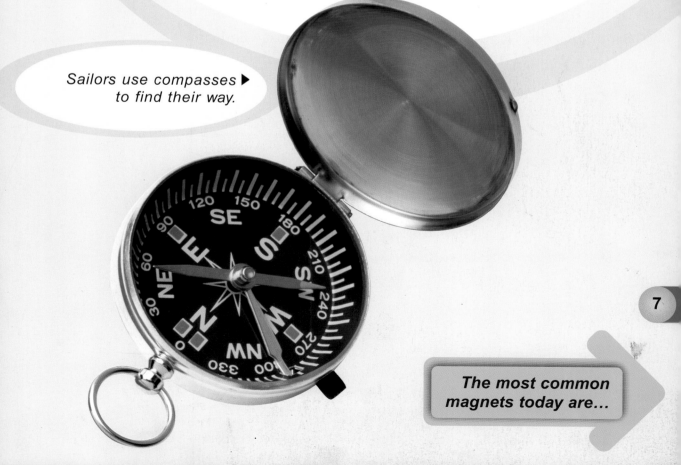

Sailors use compasses ▶ to find their way.

7

The most common magnets today are...

Fridge magnets

Do you have **magnets** on your fridge? These magnets have a small piece of **iron** on the back. They are **permanent magnets**. That means they stay **magnetic** for a long time. They keep the power of a magnet.

Fridges are not magnets. The fridge door only acts like a magnet. It does this when you put a permanent magnet on it. The door becomes a **temporary magnet**. It is only magnetic for a short time. When you remove the magnet, the door loses most of its magnetic power.

Some fridge magnets look like plastic cards. Plastic is not magnetic. Iron powder is added to the plastic. The iron turns the plastic into a permanent magnet.

What a collection!

Some people are mad about magnets! Marlou Freeman lives in Maryland in the United States. She has collected more than 2,300 fridge magnets.

permanent magnet   magnet that stays magnetized for a long time
temporary magnet   something that becomes a magnet for a short time

Powerful pullers

Another kind of **magnet** is a gripper magnet. These magnets allow workers to climb tall buildings. Scientists use **magnetism** to make gripper magnets. Magnetism is the strong pulling power of magnets.

Grippers are **permanent magnets**. They stay **magnetic** for a long time. They can turn a **steel** building into a **temporary magnet**. The building becomes magnetic for a short time. The grippers are strong enough to hold a person up.

A gripper magnet would not help you to climb a tree. It would not let you climb an icy hill. Magnets do not work on wood or ice. They only work on **iron** or steel.

Special powers

Magnets can work when they are not touching an object. Put a piece of paper between a magnet and a paper clip. Move the magnet. The paper clip will follow!

magnetism force of a magnet

▶ Spiderman? No. This man is using gripper magnets. This means he can climb tall buildings made of steel, like the ones in the big photo.

Turn the page to learn how magnets work!

One magnet, two poles

Magnets can pull things together. This is called **attraction**. It makes a magnet stick to a fridge door. It makes a gripper stick to a metal building.

Magnetic force can also keep things apart. This is called **repulsion**.

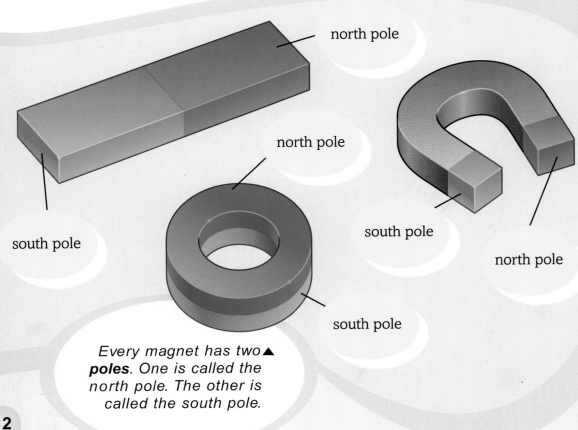

north pole

north pole

south pole

south pole

north pole

south pole

Every magnet has two ▲ poles. One is called the north pole. The other is called the south pole.

attraction   force that pulls things together

▼ *Magnets **attract** when you put a north pole near a south pole. They pull together.*

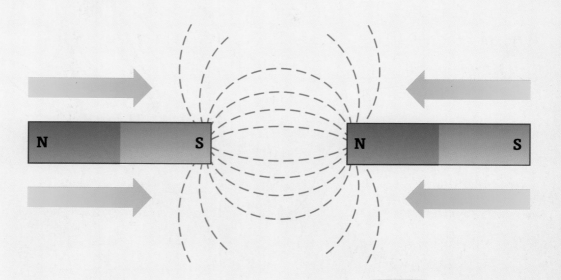

▼ *Magnets **repel** when you put two north poles together. They repel when you put two south poles together.*

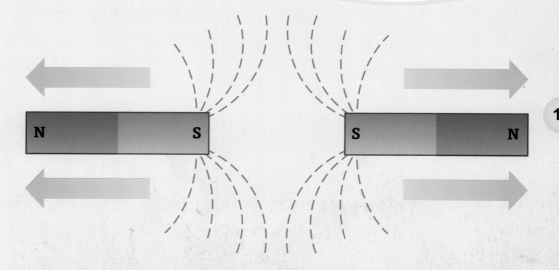

Speeding magnets

Maglev trains are the fastest trains in the world. The word *maglev* is short for "**magnetic levitation**." This means lifted by **magnets**. The trains run on **magnetism**, or the force of magnets. They lift up off the track as they move.

Maglev trains use the ▶ power of magnets.

levitation   lifting up

Maglev trains do not have wheels. There are powerful magnets on the track. These face magnets underneath the train. The magnets **repel** (push away from) each other. The magnets lift the train just above the track.

Maglev trains do not have engines. Magnets on the track **attract** (pull) magnets on the train. They pull the train forward. Maglev trains can travel at 500 kilometres (300 miles) per hour.

World's fastest train

A maglev train runs between the airport and the city of Shanghai in China. It takes only 7 minutes and 20 seconds to make the 31-kilometre (19-mile) trip.

What makes these magnets so strong?

This electromagnet can lift ▼ heavy loads when the power is on. When it is turned off, the load falls to the ground.

16

Building better magnets

Scientists have learned how to increase the power of **magnets**. They use **electricity**. This is a form of energy. Energy is the power that makes things move or work. Electricity can power machines. Magnets that work with electricity are called **electromagnets**.

Electromagnets are not **permanent magnets**. They do not stay **magnetic** for a long time. They only work when the electricity is turned on.

You need wire to make an electromagnet. Wrap a coil of wire around an **iron** bar. Turn on the electricity. The bar becomes a magnet. Turn it off. The magnet stops working.

Electromagnets are used in scrap yards. They can lift heavy loads. But they can only lift metal.

What if there were no magnets?

electricity   energy used to make heat, light, or the power to run machines

electromagnet   magnet made with electricity

Magnets at work

Without **electromagnets**, a car would not start. **Magnets** are used in all electric **motors**. A motor is a machine. It makes something move or run. Motors in your house might include:

- fridge
- telephone
- radio
- doorbell

All of these things have motors. The motors run on electromagnets.

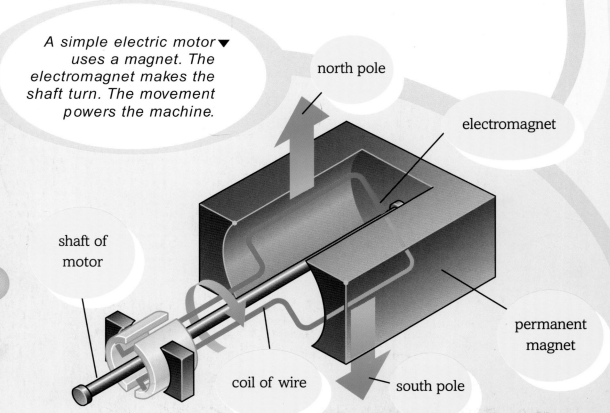

A simple electric motor ▼ uses a magnet. The electromagnet makes the shaft turn. The movement powers the machine.

north pole

electromagnet

shaft of motor

permanent magnet

coil of wire

south pole

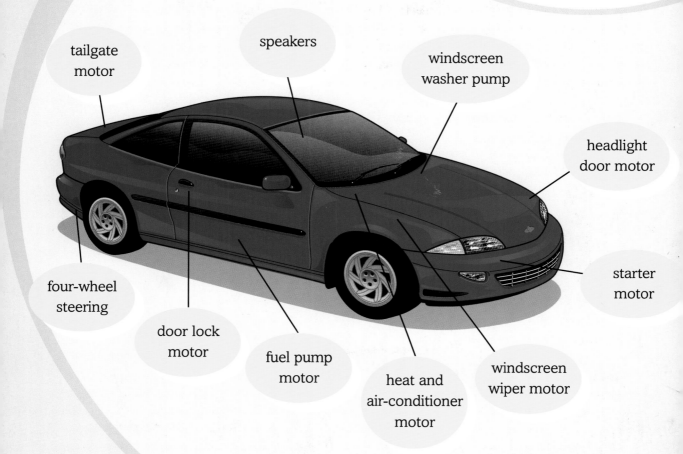

speakers

tailgate motor

windscreen washer pump

headlight door motor

four-wheel steering

starter motor

door lock motor

fuel pump motor

heat and air-conditioner motor

windscreen wiper motor

Without magnets, motors would not work. Without magnets, you would have to walk, or ride a bike. Magnets keep us moving.

motor   machine that produces energy to make something move or run

Magnets and sound

Magnets allow you to hear sounds that are far away. Sound is caused by **vibration**. Vibration is very fast backward and forward movement. Vibrations travel through the air. They reach your ears.

You can hear the sounds around you without magnets. But you cannot hear sounds that are far away. Magnets make that possible.

Electromagnets cause vibration inside speakers. As the vibrations increase, the sound gets louder. Radios and televisions use magnets to make sound. So do loudspeakers.

Getting smaller

Early magnets were large. Early radios and TVs were large too. Now we have small magnets. We can have small radios and TVs.

20

vibration very fast backward and forward movement

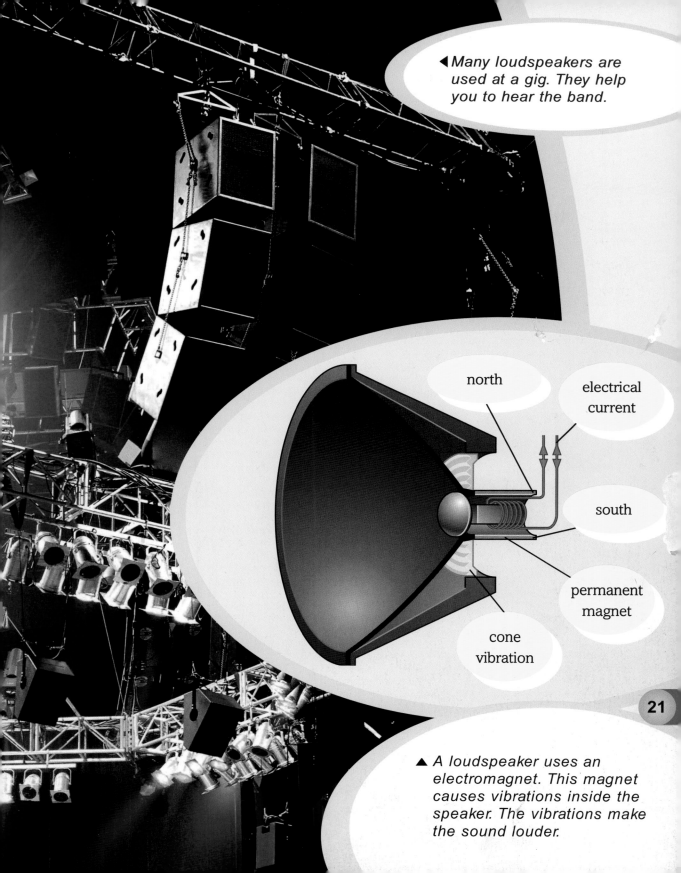

Many loudspeakers are used at a gig. They help you to hear the band.

north

electrical current

south

permanent magnet

cone vibration

▲ A loudspeaker uses an electromagnet. This magnet causes vibrations inside the speaker. The vibrations make the sound louder.

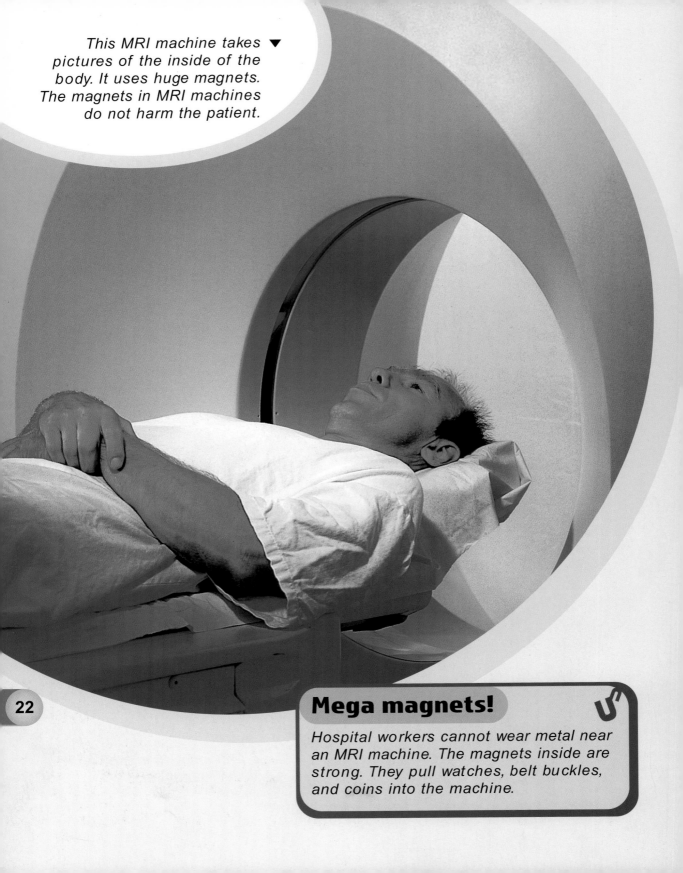

This MRI machine takes ▼ pictures of the inside of the body. It uses huge magnets. The magnets in MRI machines do not harm the patient.

Mega magnets!

Hospital workers cannot wear metal near an MRI machine. The magnets inside are strong. They pull watches, belt buckles, and coins into the machine.

Magnets to make you well

Magnets can help make people well. Doctors use **permanent magnets**. These magnets stay magnetized for a long time. They can help doctors pull a small piece of metal out of your skin. Doctors use an MRI machine to look inside a patient's body. MRI stands for "**Magnetic Resonance Imaging**". The MRI machine uses magnets to take a picture. The picture shows what is inside your body.

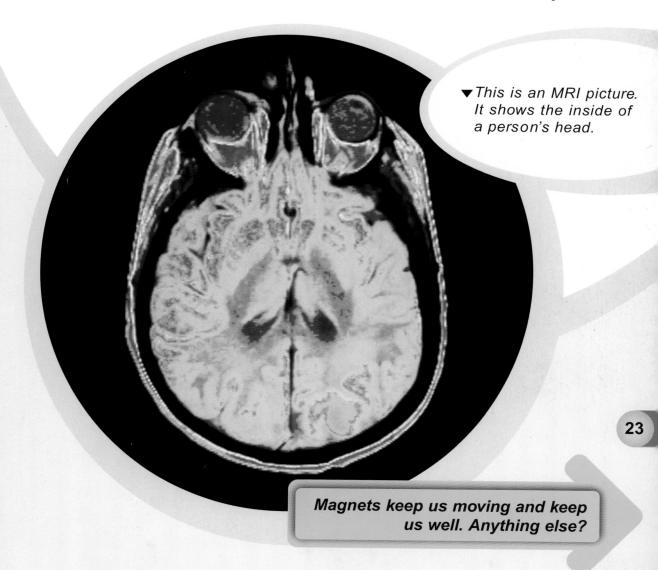

▼ *This is an MRI picture. It shows the inside of a person's head.*

Magnets keep us moving and keep us well. Anything else?

Out of this world

Magnets also work in space. Astronauts use magnets to keep everything in the right place. Without magnets, supplies would float around the spacecraft. There is no **gravity** in space. Gravity is the force that pulls us toward the ground.

Scientists sent machines called rovers into space. The rovers studied Mars. They carried **permanent magnets**. These magnets stay magnetized for a long time. They attracted **magnetic** dust. Machines on the rovers study the dust. They tell us what the surface of Mars is really like.

Electromagnets in space

Electromagnets are also useful in space. They keep some of the machines on spacecraft running. Electromagnets are used in TVs and radios. They help scientists send pictures and messages. They send them from Earth to space and back.

gravity   force that pulls us toward Earth

▼ Magnets helped the rover on Mars to collect magnetic Martian dust.

25

So, where are all the other hidden magnets?

Magnets everywhere

Magnets have many uses. You have just read about a few of them. Here are a few more:

- Telephones
- Video cameras
- Airport security machines
- Credit cards
- Toys and games
- Vending machines
- Hotel room key cards
- Science tools and machines
- Microphones

Can you think of any others?

The world would be very different without magnets. There would be no cars or buses. There would be no aeroplanes. You could not listen to music on the radio. You could not watch television.

Scientists keep finding new ways to use magnets. Magnets help make our lives safer and easier.

27

Magnet power

Magnets are everywhere. They have amazing powers to **attract** or **repel**. Think about magnets the next time you play a video game. Think about them when you watch TV. Magnets make your world a better place!

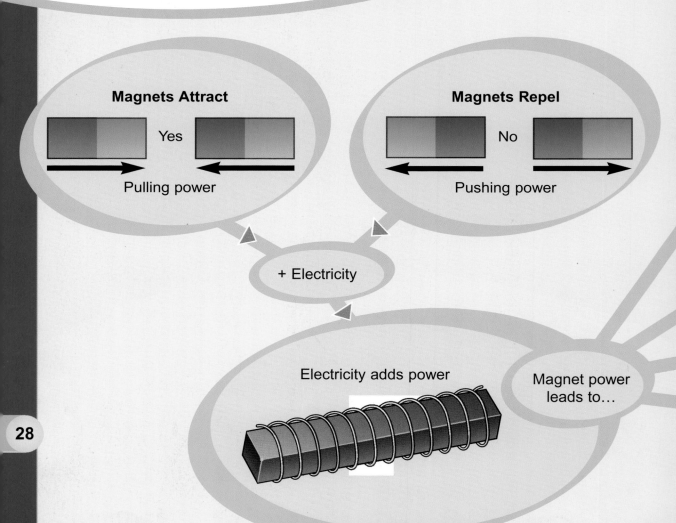

Magnets Attract

Yes

Pulling power

Magnets Repel

No

Pushing power

+ Electricity

Electricity adds power

Magnet power leads to...

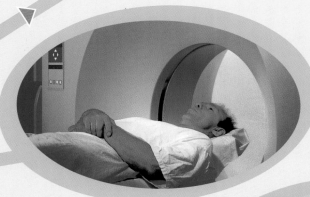

Glossary

attract pull together. Two unlike magnetic poles attract.

attraction force that pulls things together, such as the unlike poles of a magnet

compass tool that uses magnetism to find direction. Bring a compass if you are walking in the forest.

electricity energy used to make heat, light, or the power to run machines. Electromagnets use electricity.

electromagnet magnet made with electricity. You can turn an electromagnet on and off.

gravity force that pulls us towards Earth

iron bright, silver-coloured metal. Most magnets are made of iron.

levitation lifting up. The maglev train uses magnetic levitation to make it run.

lodestone rock that is a natural magnet. Ancient sailors used lodestones as compasses.

magnet object with the power to attract things made of iron, steel, nickel, or cobalt. Most magnets are made of iron.

magnetic something that has the power of a magnet. Some of the dust on Mars is magnetic.

magnetism force of a magnet. Magnetism is a powerful force.

motor machine that produces energy to make something move or run. All motors use magnetism.

permanent magnet magnet that stays magnetized for a long time. A lodestone is a permanent magnet.

pole part of a magnet that seeks the north or south pole of Earth. Every magnet has a north pole and a south pole.

repel push away. Two north poles repel each other.

repulsion force that pushes things apart

steel hard, tough metal that contains iron. Many office buildings are made of steel.

temporary magnet something that becomes a magnet for a short time. A fridge door becomes a temporary magnet when you put a magnet on it.

vibration very fast backward and forward movement. Speakers use vibration to make noises louder.

Want to know more?

Books to read

- *Horrible Science: Killer Energy and Shocking Electricity*, by Nick Arnold (Scholastic, 2006)

- *Routes of Science: Gravity*, by Chris Woodford (Blackbirch, 2004)

- *Tabletop Scientist: Electricity and Magnetism*, Steve Parker (Heinemann Library 2005)

Websites

- http://www.exploratorium.edu/snacks/iconmagnetism.html

  Find out about some more experiments you can do with magnets.

- http://liftoff.msfc.nasa.gov/News/1999/News-MagLev.asp

  Check out this website to learn more about launching rockets with magnets.

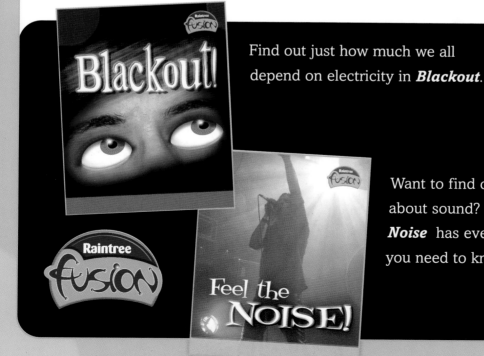

Find out just how much we all depend on electricity in *Blackout*.

Want to find out more about sound? *Feel the Noise* has everything you need to know.

Index

airport security machines 26

astronauts 24

attraction 4, 12, 13, 15, 28

cars 18, 19, 27

compasses 6

credit cards 26

electricity 17, 21

electromagnets 16, 17, 18, 20,
   21, 24

gravity 24

gripper magnets 10–11

iron 4, 7, 8, 10

key cards 26

lodestones 6, 7

loudspeakers 20, 21

maglev trains 14–15, 17

magnetic dust 24, 25

magnetic levitation 14

magnetism 10, 14

Mars 24, 25

metals 4, 7, 10, 17

microphones 26

motors 18, 19

Mr. Magnet 4, 5

MRI machines 22, 23

permanent magnets 8, 10, 17, 21,
   23, 24

plastic 8

poles 12, 13

radios and televisions 20, 24, 27

repulsion 12, 13, 15, 28

rovers 24, 25

scrap yards 17

sound 20–21

space exploration 24–25

spacecraft 24

steel 4, 10

telephones 26

temporary magnets 8, 10

toys and games 26

vending machines 26

vibrations 20, 21

video cameras 26